#		Page
1.	Script Kiddies Have Little Hacking Experience	5
2.	Script Kiddies Use Premade Tools	8
3.	Script Kiddies Are the Lowest Level of Hackers	11
4.	Script Kiddies Hack for Fun or Out of Curiosity	14
5.	Script Kiddies Can Get into Big Legal Trouble	17
6.	Script Kiddies Don't Hide Their Tracks Well	21
7.	Cybersecurity Pros Know the Signs of an Attack	24
8.	Script Kiddies Can Be the Worst Threat	27
9.	Most Skiddies Start Out by Hacking Alone	30
10.	Script Kiddies Often Target Online Gamers	34
11.	Make Yourself a Hard Target for Skiddies	37
12.	Learn to Hack the "Right" Way	40
	Fact Sheet	44
	Glossary	46
	For More Information	47
	Index	48

Hacking takes a lot of computer skills and knowledge, two things script kiddies often lack.

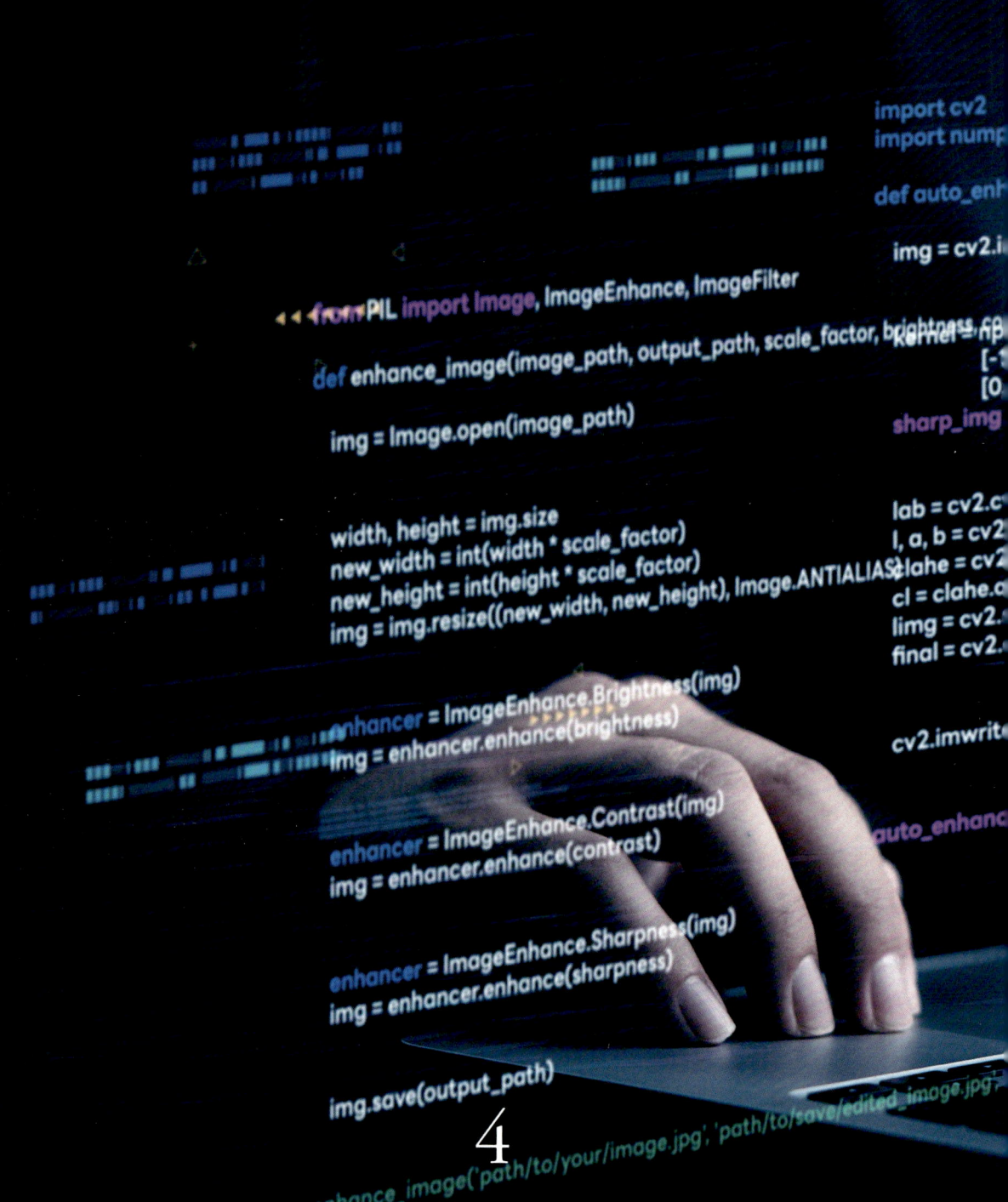

Script Kiddies Have Little *Hacking Experience*

Not all hackers are experts. Some are beginners. They don't know how computers or code really work. These people are called script kiddies. Sometimes it's shortened to "skid" or "skiddies." The word "kid" refers to the level of experience someone has in the hacker space. It's not a nice name. It usually means someone is trying to hack without putting in the work. They haven't learned the right skills.

Script kiddies often skip learning how to code. They don't know much about networks or **cybersecurity**. Instead of studying, they try things over and over until something works. This is called "trial and error."

Some script kiddies want to become better hackers. But most give up. Becoming a good hacker is hard. You spend a lot of time learning how everything works. You learn about computers, websites, and security systems. You need to know how to write code. You must test systems.

Hacking is not just about pressing buttons. It's about thinking, learning, and solving puzzles. You can't just copy someone else's work. Script kiddies often miss this. That's why skilled hackers don't respect them.

Some hackers start as script kiddies. But they stick with it. They work hard to learn and grow. They grasp how to hack safely and legally. These people can become strong ethical hackers. They can help protect others.

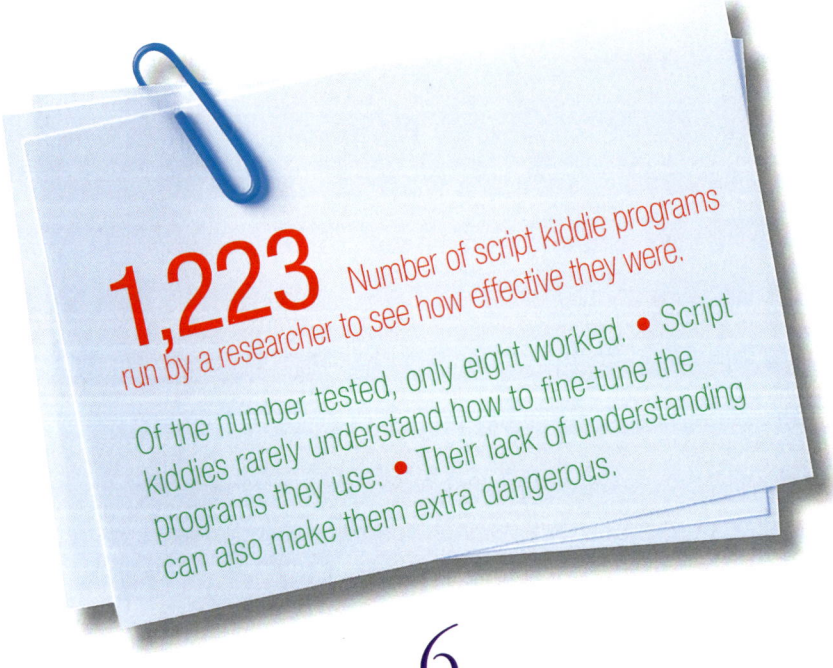

1,223 Number of script kiddie programs run by a researcher to see how effective they were. • Of the number tested, only eight worked. • Script kiddies rarely understand how to fine-tune the programs they use. • Their lack of understanding can also make them extra dangerous.

FIRST 5CR1P7 K1DD13S

No one really knows where "script kiddie" came from. As the internet grew, more people joined online. They formed communities. In hacker communities, they used numbers and symbols in place of letters. It was like an online form of slang. Terms for someone using code they didn't understand started to emerge. They were called 5cr1p7 k1dd1e, sk1d, skiddy, scriptkid, and skript kiddy. Today they are called script kiddies.

Kids who learn the basics of coding can become great hackers.

Script Kiddies Use *Premade Tools*

2

Script kiddies don't build their own tools. Instead, they use tools made by other hackers. These tools are called **scripts**. You can find them in online forums or websites.

These tools can break into weak websites or systems. But there's a problem. Script kiddies often don't understand how the tools work. They just copy and paste them. That's why they are sometimes called "copy-paste hackers."

Script kiddies make lots of mistakes. Sometimes their hacks don't work. Other times, they hurt their own computers! They might download a tool that's actually a **virus**. They might mess up the code and cause errors.

Script kiddies love shortcuts. But hacking isn't about shortcuts. It's about learning. Skilled hackers used tools too. Tools can save time. But they must be used right.

Script kiddies often copy and paste codes they don't fully understand.

40 Estimated percent of script kiddies who use premade tools without knowing how they work.

It is impossible to know the exact number of these kinds of attacks. • These attacks can cause a lot of damage. • AI has made it easier for people to create scripts they don't understand.

In the hands of someone unskilled, these tools can be dangerous. That's why it's better to learn how things work instead of just copying code.

Coding is like learning a new language. There are those who know a few words. They only understand words in a specific setting. Those who are fluent have a much wider knowledge. They can create connections. People who know code well can build their own tools. They can help other people. Being curious about hacking is great. But don't start by copying things you don't understand. Instead, learn how things work. You'll go a lot further.

Programmers begin by learning code.

Script Kiddies Are the Lowest Level of Hackers

3

Imagine hackers are in a big pyramid. At the top are smart, skilled hackers. They know what they are doing, whether for good or bad intent. In the middle are people who are learning. At the very bottom are script kiddies. This is where most people start.

Script kiddies don't know much about hacking. They don't write their own code or understand how systems work. Instead, they use other people's tools. They try things without thinking. Other hackers look down on them. Skiddies may brag about what they do. They often act like they are really good, but they are not. Because of this, experienced hackers don't respect them.

Hackers are often judged by what they know and why they hack. Some hackers try to help people. Some want to hurt others or steal things. Script kiddies are somewhere in the middle. They don't always mean harm. But they also don't know enough to help.

Script kiddies are easy to spot. They don't know how to hide their identity online. They don't use special tools to cover their tracks. That makes it easy to catch them. They often don't understand the law. They sometimes break it without realizing it.

Not all script kiddies stay at the bottom. Some work hard to improve. With enough practice and effort, they can move up. They can become real cybersecurity experts.

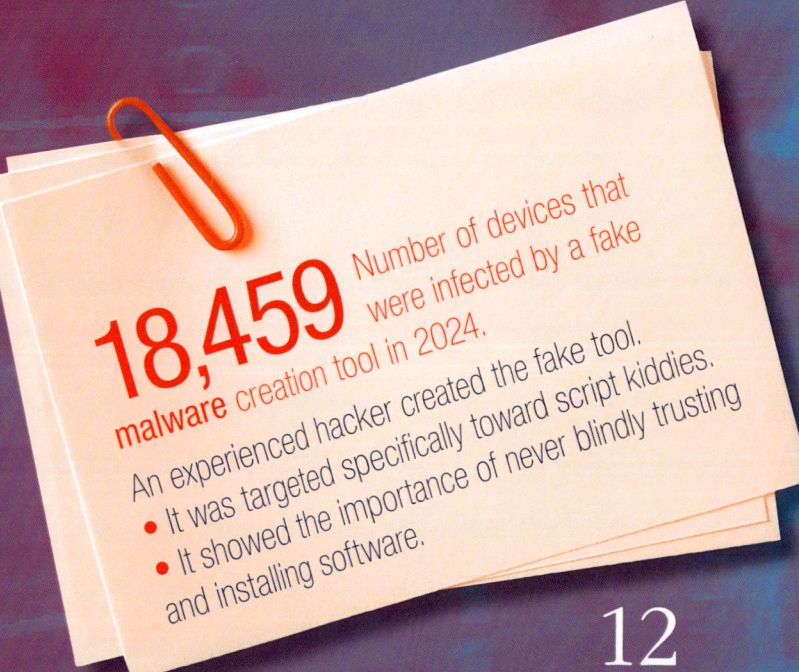

18,459 Number of devices that were infected by a fake malware creation tool in 2024.

- An experienced hacker created the fake tool.
- It was targeted specifically toward script kiddies.
- It showed the importance of never blindly trusting and installing software.

Think About It
Have you ever downloaded a game or a file online? Did it come from a trusted site? How did you know you could trust it was real?

Script kiddies have just enough knowledge to make them dangerous.

Script Kiddies
Hack for Fun or *Out of Curiosity*

4

Some script kiddies aren't trying to be mean. They are just curious. They want to see what happens when they run a code or push a button. Many start by using cheat codes in video games. Later, they might wonder. What else can you do with coding? They are led by curiosity.

Skiddies might try small hacks. They try to guess someone's password. Or they try breaking into a website. They often don't know how serious this can be. One example is a teen from Canada. He used a script to crash several school websites. He thought it was funny. But he got in big trouble. What he did was against the law.

Script kiddies often go after easy targets. These are websites that haven't been updated in a long time. Or they are accounts with weak passwords. They don't

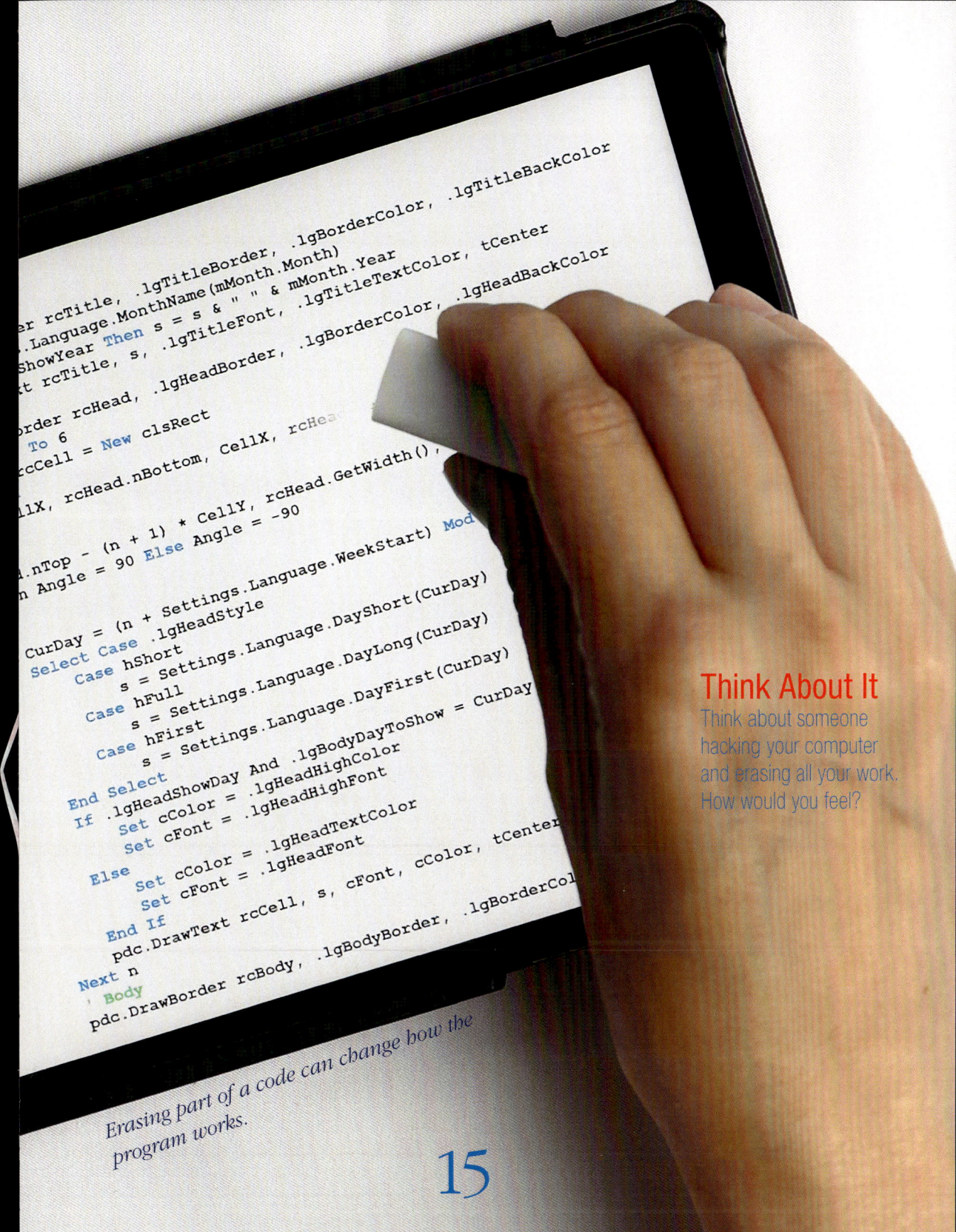

Erasing part of a code can change how the program works.

Think About It
Think about someone hacking your computer and erasing all your work. How would you feel?

usually stop to think, "Is this right?" or "Will this hurt someone?" They just want to see what happens. But hacking for fun can still cause a lot of problems.

If you're interested in computers, there are safe ways to explore. You can learn how websites work. Join a coding club. Or play ethical hacking games. Then you can be curious *and* helpful!

37 Seconds it takes to crack a password made of eight numbers.

Script kiddies use "brute force" tools to guess passwords. • These tools try many combinations of characters until one works. • A password with a mix of 8 characters would take seven years to crack.

MAKE THE RIGHT DECISION

Script Kiddies Can Get into Big Legal Trouble

Script kiddies may think they are playing around. But they may be breaking the law. Hacking a website, crashing a game, or stealing someone's account is not "goofing off." These are crimes. One big problem? Script kiddies don't always understand what they're doing. They run scripts they find online. But they don't read the code or learn what it really does. That's dangerous. It's like using a tool without reading the instructions. Things can go very wrong very fast.

Breaking the law has real consequences. You can get kicked out of school. You can lose access to the internet. You might even go to jail. And once you are in trouble, it's hard to fix your record. That's why it is important to stop and think. Check if what you are doing is legal. Double check any hacking tools before using them. Ask yourself some questions. Do I know what this script does? Is this legal? If the answer is no, don't run it.

There's some good news. There are better ways to learn about hacking. You can study computer science. Join a robotics club. Or take part in Capture the Flag (CTF) games. These are online hacking games where you solve puzzles. You can find bugs in systems the right way. Some companies even reward kids for doing this! Learning to hack legally is not just smart. It can be fun. And it keeps you out of trouble.

Hacking illegally can lead to someone getting arrested.

HACKING AS A CAREER

Ethical hackers are good hackers who help protect computers and websites. They find weak spots before bad hackers can attack. Companies hire them to test security and fix problems. Ethical hackers follow the law. They use their skills for good. They make the internet safer against cybercrime.

Script Kiddies Don't Hide *Their Tracks Well*

6

When skilled hackers do something bad, they try to hide it. They use special tools and tricks to cover their tracks. This makes it hard for anyone to know who did it. Script kiddies, on the other hand, usually don't know how to do that.

There are many ways hackers try to hide their identity. One way is encryption. It turns data into a secret code. Another way is steganography. This hides a message inside a picture or file. Some hackers use VPNs. They make it look like they are in another country. Others may use **obfuscation**. This scrambles code so it is harder to understand.

Script kiddies don't usually hide their identity. They often leave behind clues, like their real location or username. It's like leaving your name and address after breaking into someone's house. You'd be easy to catch!

Because of this, script kiddies are often the first ones caught when there's a cyberattack. They don't take time to cover their steps.

If you go into cybersecurity, you don't need to hide who you are. But it is helpful to learn how others do it. It helps to understand how attackers work. Then you know how to stop them. That's why experts study these tools. This way, they can protect people from harm.

19 Average age of someone charged with cybercrime in the United States.

This young age proves script kiddies are more likely to get caught. • Some skiddies get arrested before they even finish high school. • Computer hackers can be any age.

Information left behind after online activity is part of a person's digital footprint.

Cybersecurity Pros Know the Signs *of an Attack*

Script kiddies think they are sneaky. But experts can often tell when they have been attacked by one. Why? Script kiddies leave behind clues. Most script kiddies use well-known tools. These scripts have patterns and names. Cybersecurity professionals know these. It's easy to spot an **LOIC** attack or a common script to steal passwords.

Script kiddies don't plan very well. A skilled hacker might leave a **ransom** note. They might hide inside a system for a long time. A script kiddie usually runs a script. They crash the website, then leave. They don't even try to hide who they are.

Their attacks are also simple and messy. They might just change the words on a website or make something crash. These are called "immature" attacks. They don't

take much effort or skill. Sometimes, script kiddies even brag about their hacks online. They post pictures or write about what they did. This makes them even easier to catch.

Cybersecurity teams look for these signs. They check for common scripts, sloppy coding, or attacks with no real purpose. Once they find them, they can trace the attack. They find the person who did it. That's why hacking without knowing what you're doing is risky. Script kiddies are the easiest hackers to catch. If you want to work in cybersecurity someday, it's better to learn the right way. Then you will be the one stopping the attacks instead of causing them.

35 million Number of devices targeted by a script kiddie known as Matrix.

• Matrix created a botnet to launch huge **DDoS** attacks. • Botnets use open-source tools to hack into network routers, cameras, and more. • Matrix is an example of how a script kiddie can cause a lot of damage.

Script Kiddies Can Be the *Worst Threat*

You might think script kiddies are harmless. They seem like pranksters. But many experts say they are dangerous hackers. Why? Their lack of knowledge is a huge threat. They could crash a website or online store without even knowing it. They could ruin a school's system or knock out a hospital's computers by accident. They don't usually plan their attacks. They just click and run a tool. But that can still cause serious damage.

Script kiddies also make a lot of mistakes. They might run the same attack again and again, hoping it works. That can crash **servers**. It makes systems unusable.

Script kiddies also spread harmful tools. When they find a script that works, they often share it with others. They post it in forms and online chats. This creates a market for bad tools. Suddenly, a simple script is being used by hundreds of people.

Even if a script kiddie doesn't mean to hurt anyone, their actions can lead to big problems. That's why some experts work hard to block their attacks. They teach kids that hacking the wrong way can be dangerous. Become part of the solution instead. Learn how things work. Think before you click. This will help build a safer internet for everyone.

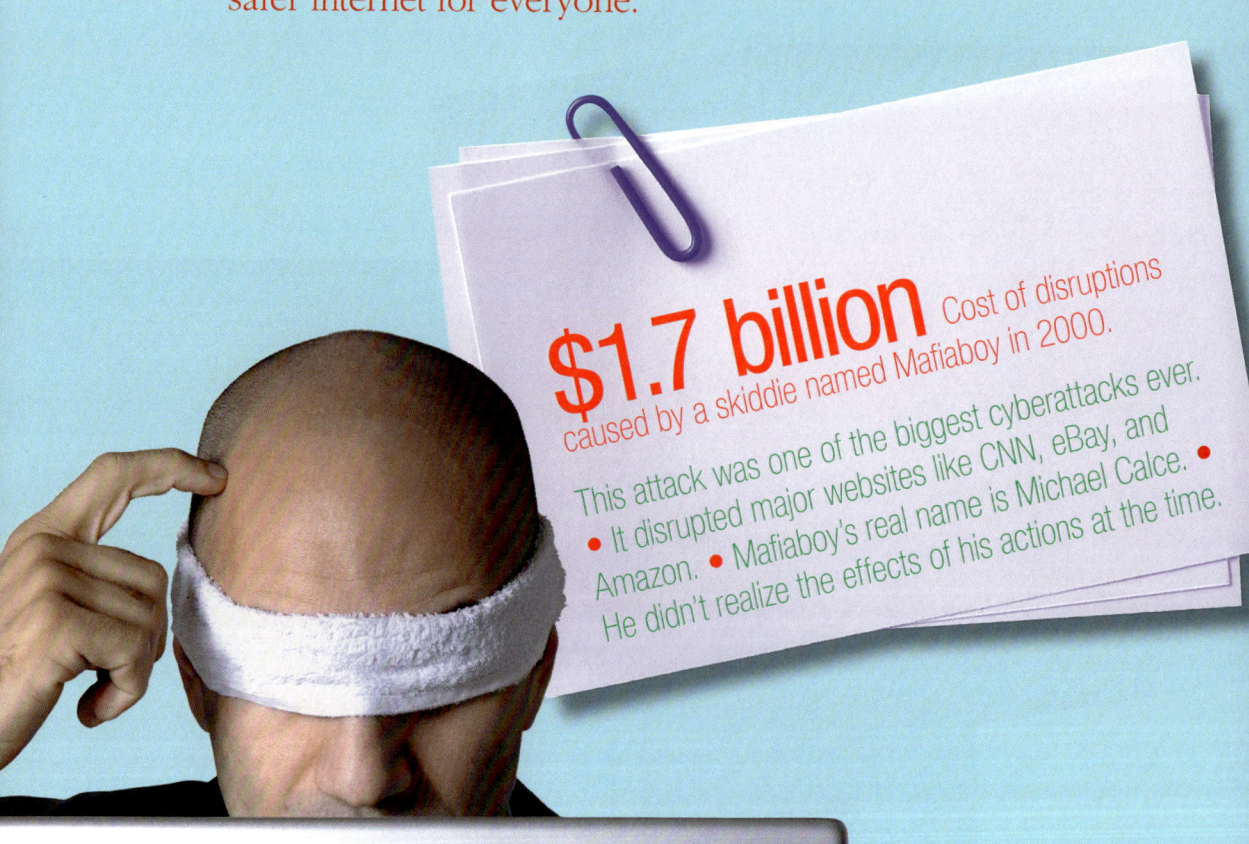

$1.7 billion Cost of disruptions caused by a skiddie named Mafiaboy in 2000.

- This attack was one of the biggest cyberattacks ever.
- It disrupted major websites like CNN, eBay, and Amazon.
- Mafiaboy's real name is Michael Calce. He didn't realize the effects of his actions at the time.

Skiddies are unpredictable due to their lack of knowledge.

HIDDEN INTERNET Script kiddies sometimes visit the **dark web**. This is a secret online space. Hackers can find tools, stolen passwords, and join shady forums. Skiddies often don't know how dangerous it is. Many download fake or harmful programs. They get tricked. Or they reveal their identity. Using the dark web can lead to serious trouble.

Most Skiddies Start Out by *Hacking Alone*

9

Many cybercriminals work in groups. But script kiddies usually work alone. They don't plan big attacks or lead teams. Most of them find tools online. They try them out and hope something happens. They often visit forums where hackers talk and share scripts. Some have step-by-step guides. They are easy to use. But they don't explain how anything works. Skiddies just copy, paste, and press "go."

Because they're alone, script kiddies don't always have someone to help them or teach them. They make mistakes. They leave clues. And when things go wrong, they don't know how to fix them.

Some script kiddies want to improve. They want to stop being called "kiddies" and start being respected. To do that, they join online groups that focus on learning. Some join hacker collectives. These teams of people share knowledge. They grow their skills together. Others join groups using Discord or other apps. People help each other learn ethical hacking.

If you're curious about hacking, it's better to learn with a group. Find one that wants to help, not just attack. Some teams fix security bugs or solve puzzles. Being part of a team is more fun and useful. Even if you start solo, you don't have to stay there. With effort, anyone can become an expert.

Think About It
When is learning as a team better than learning alone?

28,433 Number of Discord servers in August 2024.

Discord is a free app. • People can communicate in groups called servers. • Most servers are for gaming. • But many others focus on education and technology.

Script Kiddies Often Target *Online Gamers*

10

Many games and gamers have weak security. That makes them easy targets for script kiddies. Skiddies often target these gaming communities. Some use tools like LOIC to crash game servers. They send too many signals at once. The game freezes or goes offline. They might do it to slow down rivals. Or they just want to cause chaos.

Other skiddies try to steal accounts. If you use the same password a lot, they might guess it. They can take over your account. Some script kiddies even sell cheats for games. But the cheats include viruses that infect your device.

Why do they do these attacks? Sometimes it is for revenge on other gamers. Sometimes they are bored. And sometimes they just want attention. No matter the reason, it's not fair to the people who just want to play.

UP IN THE CLOUD Have you ever played a game on multiple devices? Maybe you started playing on a tablet. Then you switched to a phone or a laptop. Did you notice that your progress moved with you? That's because your game is saving your information in the cloud. The cloud is made up of servers that store data. Saving data to the cloud can be handy. But it also makes it easier for others to steal your data.

Gaming companies work hard to block these attacks. Gamers can help too. If you play games online, protect your account. Use a strong, unique password. Don't download cheats or hacks from strangers. And tell an adult or game moderator if something feels wrong. Being a smart gamer keeps you safe. It keeps the fun going for everyone else.

Cheat codes are often used in first-person shooter games.

167 Percentage increase in cyberattacks on gaming in 2022.

The United States is the main target for attacks. Next, Switzerland and India are the most attacked. • Games often use **cloud storage**. This is a remote place to store data. • Hackers are targeting the cloud more and more.

Make Yourself a Hard Target *for Skiddies*

11

You can protect yourself from script kiddies. Most of the time, they look for easy targets. They only attack people or websites that are easy to hack. The same goes for more skilled hackers as well. Protecting yourself will prevent most attacks. If you follow smart safety steps, they'll move on.

Password security is one of the best things you can do. Plus it's a quick and easy step. Use strong passwords. Don't use "123456" or "password." Try a mix of letters, numbers, and symbols. Never reuse passwords. Every account should have its own.

To protect your devices, turn on automatic updates. This helps keep your software safe and up to date. Be careful with downloads. Only get files or apps from places you trust. Script kiddies aren't elite hackers. They look for lazy mistakes. If your computer or game account is protected, they'll have a harder time hacking you.

A lot of hacking depends on human error. Someone may click the wrong link or fall for a scam. If you're ever unsure, ask a parent or teacher. It's better to ask than to get tricked. The more you learn about cybersecurity, the harder you'll be to hack. Then you can help others stay safe too.

15 billion Number of usernames and passwords available for sale online.

A hacker may try to break into an account using the same username and password stolen from another site. • Script kiddies and other hackers use bots to try millions of stolen logins quickly. • This is why it's important to try not to reuse passwords.

A unique password is the best way to protect yourself.

Think About It
Go through all your accounts. Are you using the same passwords in multiple places? Think of a new, stronger password for each account. Make sure it is unique to that account.

Learn to Hack the *"Right" Way*

12

If you're curious about hacking, that's great! But there's a right way to do it. Hacking doesn't have to mean breaking the law. In fact, some hackers are superheroes for the internet. They help stop the bad guys and fix problems. These ethical hackers use their skills to protect others. And the fun part? You can learn to do that too.

If you want to become an ethical hacker, you need to learn to code. Start with fun websites like Scratch. Or try a simple programming language like Python. It is also helpful to know how computers are built. Study robotics or hardware. Learn how these devices work. Play cybersecurity games. There are puzzles called CTFs (Capture the Flag) where you practice safe hacking. Join bug bounty programs. Some companies pay you to find problems in their websites. And it's legal.

Finally, talk to people who work in the field. Find teachers, clubs, or online groups that teach ethical hacking. Hacking doesn't need to be sneaky. It can be about problem solving and thinking like a detective. Mostly, it can help keep others safe. That's how you go from script kiddie to cybersecurity superhero.

Hackers learn many coding languages, their strengths, weaknesses, and what each is best used for.

8 Youngest age for several websites with hacking challenges.

Search for "hackchallengesforkids.com" to learn about hacking. • Professional sites like HackerOne and HackTheBox require users to be at least 13. • These sites are a great starting point to learn about cybersecurity and hacking.

Games can challenge kids to learn to hack in new ways.

Index

attitude, 6, 8, 11, 14, 17

botnets, 26, 38
bugs, 18, 31, 40

cheat codes, 14, 34, 36
coding, 5, 6, 8, 10, 11, 14, 16, 26, 40
cyberattacks, 9, 22, 24, 26, 27, 28, 34, 36
    DDoS, 26
    clues, 21, 24, 30
    LOIC, 24, 34
cybercrime, 17, 20, 22, 45
cybersecurity, 5, 12, 22, 24, 26, 38, 40, 41, 42, 44

dark web, 29

ethical hackers, 6, 16, 20, 31, 40–41

games, 16, 18, 40

hacker groups, 30–31, 41
hiding, 12, 21–22, 24

laws, 12, 14, 17, 20, 40
learning to hack, 5, 6, 8, 10, 18, 22, 28, 30–31, 40–41, 42, 45

Mafiaboy, 28
malware, 12
Matrix, 26

name origin, 5

passwords, 14, 16, 24, 29, 34, 36, 37, 38, 39
programs, 6, 29

scripts, 8, 9, 14, 17, 18, 24, 26, 27, 30, 44
servers, 27, 33, 34, 35
skills, 6, 31, 40, 44

targets, 12, 14, 26, 34, 37

video games, 14, 17, 34, 35, 36
viruses, 8, 34

TOP RANK is published by Black Rabbit Books, P.O. Box 227, Mankato, MN, 56002. • Copyright © 2026 Black Rabbit Books. All rights reserved. No part of this book may be reproduced in any form without written permission from the publisher. • Designed by Danny Nanos • Photographs © Dreamstime/Cammeraydave, 44; Getty Images/Bill Hinton, 29, bubaone, 23, Grafissimo, 11, imaginima, cover, 1; Shutterstock/Africa Studio, 8, AndreasG, 2–3, 25, Andrii Zastrozhnov, 18, Antlii, 41, Artem Onoprienko, 19, axpitel, 43, Belinda Pretorius, 48, Bits And Splits, 39, breakermaximus, 36, Cheer Group, 34, Diego Thomazini, 31, enterlinedesign, 24, Foundation EQM, 14, Gts, 45, Gus Andrade, 28, Hsyn20, 44, Jirik V, 38, Jirsak, 35, Jolygon, 46–47, khunkornStudio, 4–5, Lisa F. Young, 21, Luis Molinero, 2, 13, Max_Z, 15, metamorworks, 42–43, Natali _ Mis, 9, Navorolphotography, 30, New Africa, 37, ozrimoz, 12–13, Raland, 32–33, Rob Hyrons, 22, Roman Samborskyi, 45, RT Design Studio, 26, RTimages, 16, StepanPopov, 27, Summit Art Creations, 7, TimeStopper69, 10, VRVIRUS, 20, Wright Studio, 40; Wikimedia Commons/Vin Louisel, 2 • Printed in the United States of America.

Library of Congress Cataloging-in-Publication Data is filed under LCCN 2025021470. ISBN 978-1-64582-524-1 (library binding), ISBN 978-1-64582-542-5 (paperback), ISBN 978-1-64582-560-9 (ebook)